MONSTER MATH

MONSTER PATTERNS

WRITTEN BY

MADELINE TYLER

ILLUSTRATED BY

AMY LI

Lerner Publications ◆ Minneapolis

First American edition published in 2020 by Lerner Publishing Group, Inc.

© 2019 Booklife Publishing
This edition is published by arrangement with Booklife Publishing.
All rights reserved.

Editor: John Wood
Design: Amy Li

Lerner Publications Company
An imprint of Lerner Publishing Group, Inc.
241 First Avenue North
Minneapolis, MN 55401 USA

For reading levels and more information, look up this title at www.lernerbooks.com.

Main body text set in Slappy Inline. Typeface provided by T26.

Photo credits:
All images courtesy of Shutterstock. With thanks to Getty Images, Thinkstock Photo and iStockphoto. Cover, Page 1 & Page 2 – memphisslim, jojje, Dmitrijj Skorobogatov, Abscent, ag1100. Master Images – jojje (grid), Dmitrijj Skorobogatov (illustration texture), Abscent (pattern), ag1100 (paper texture), Hajrudin Hodzic (wood texture) Corey Frey (Patch and monster texture), Amy Li (all illustrations). Bead patterns – Anne Punch (green square), Ilya Bolotov (peach round), stuckmotion (orange round), uiliaaa (red round). String – Pawel Michalowski, tam_odin, Ivaylo Ivanov. Bead box – Draw_wing_Zen, ag1100. Patch's Room (p3, 9, 13, 17, 21) – cluckva, Max Krasnov (wallpaper), Hajrudin Hodzic (wood texture), Africa Studio (red spool), grocap (string spool). p10 – M Kunz, p13 – M Kunz, p14 – TYSB, p18 – Natailia K,
p23 – arigato, Evgenii Iaroshevskii

Library of Congress Cataloging-in-Publication Data
The Cataloging-in-Publication Data for Monster Patterns is on file at the Library of Congress.
ISBN 978-1-5415-7929-3 (lib. bdg.)
ISBN 978-1-5415-8921-6 (pbk.)
ISBN 978-1-5415-8331-3 (eb pdf)

Manufactured in the United States of America
1-47211-47916-8/29/2019

Patch wants to make necklaces for all her friends.

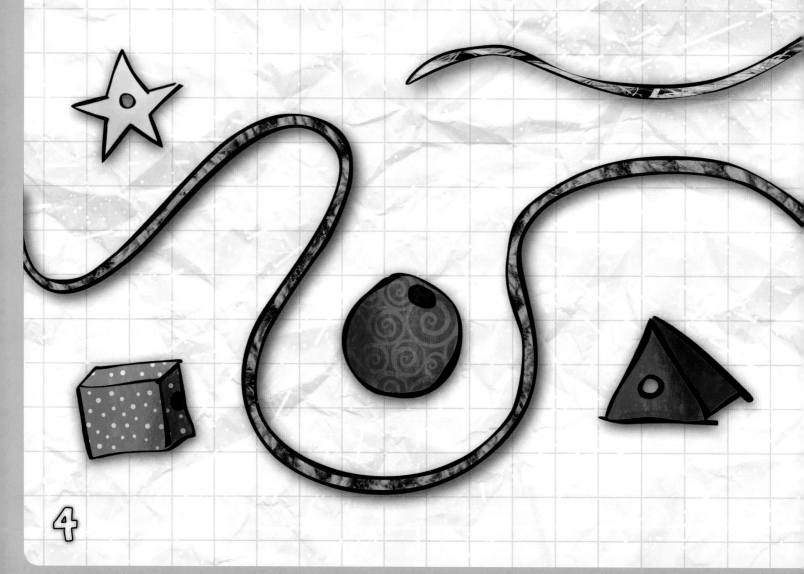

She will need lots of
beads and lots of string...

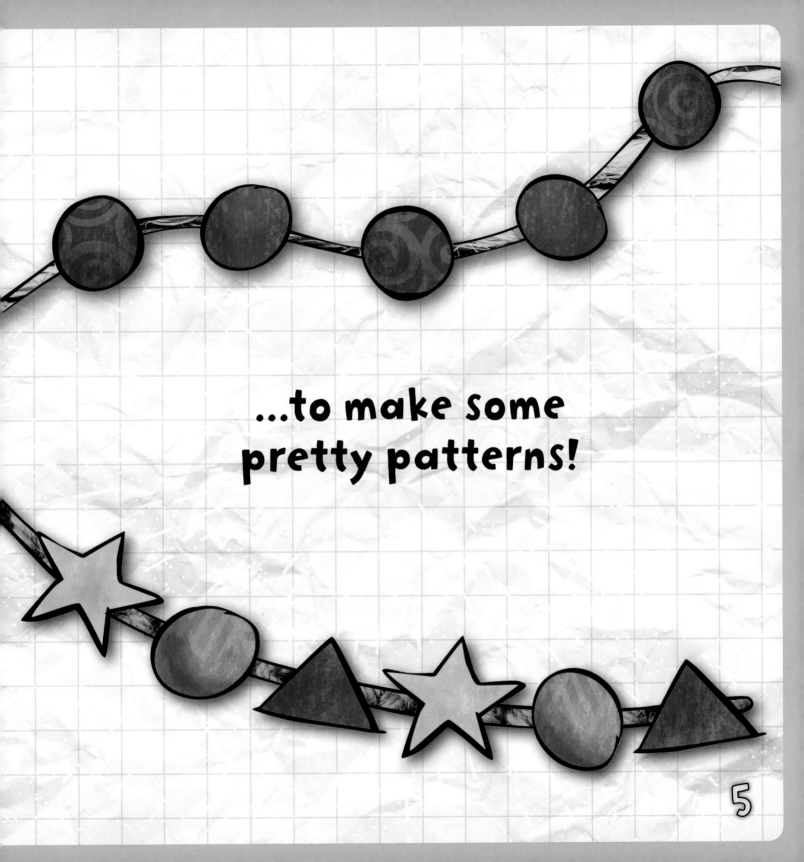

...to make some
pretty patterns!

5

Red, blue, red, blue, red...

6

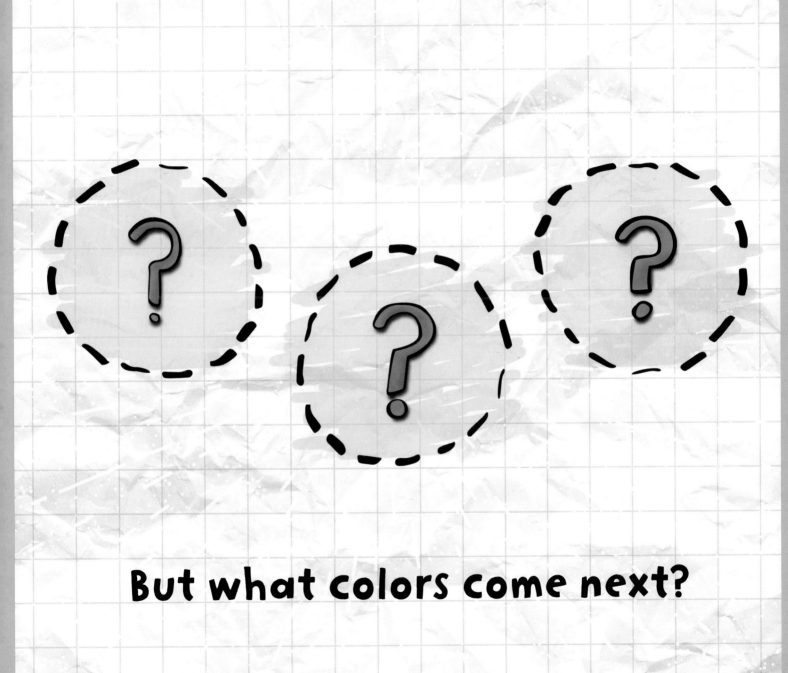

But what colors come next?

Blue, red, blue!

What a pretty pattern!

Circle, square,
circle, square...

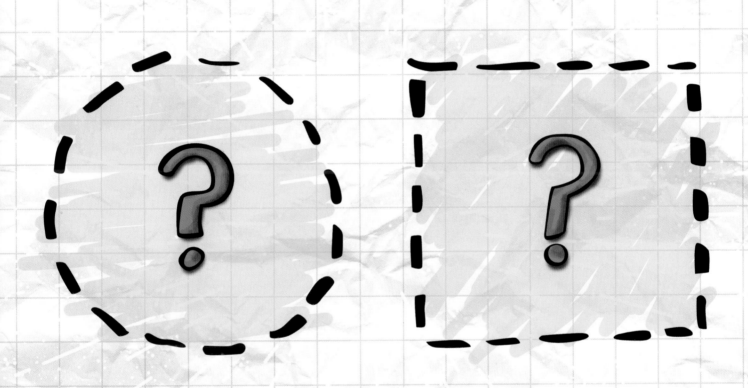

How do we finish the pattern?

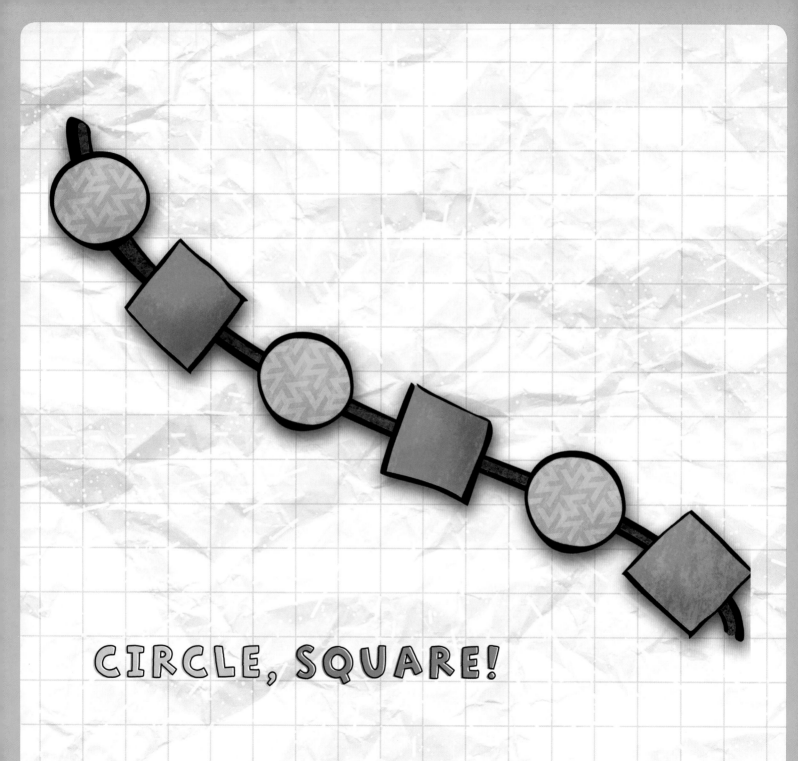

CIRCLE, SQUARE!

12

Now the necklace is finished!

Pink, pink, green,
pink, pink, green...

14

What comes after this?

15

PINK, PINK, GREEN!

What bright colors!

Beads

17

Beads

Star, circle, triangle,
star, circle, triangle...

Can you finish the pattern?

STAR, CIRCLE, TRIANGLE!

How many shapes do you see in this pattern?

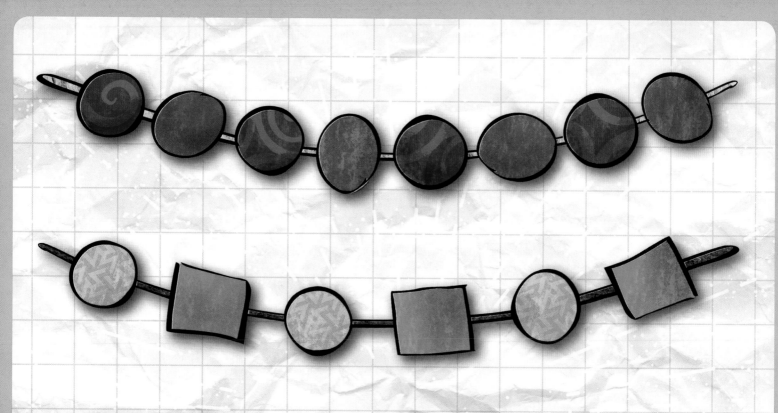

Look at those patterns!

Patch's friends love
their new necklaces!

23

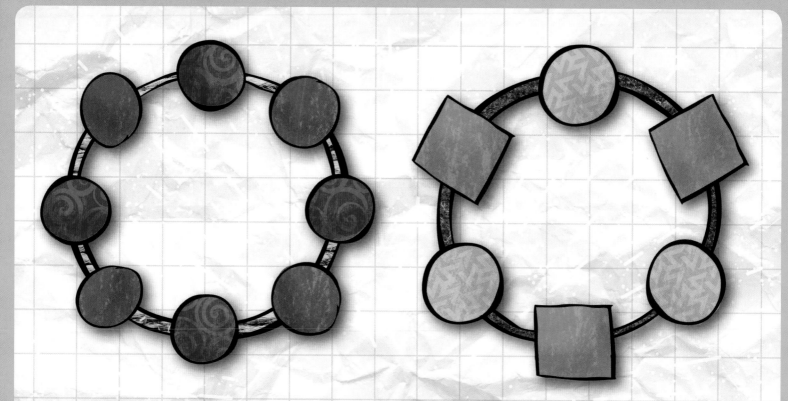

Which pattern would you choose?

24